Michele D. Allen B.A.
No part of this publication may be reproduced in whole or in part, or stored in a retrieval system, or transmitted in any form by any means, electronic, mechanical, photocopying, recording, or otherwise, without written permission of the publisher.

Copyright © 2022 by Michele D. Allen B.A.
All rights reserved, Published by Digital D'zines & Publish

Daughter's Bestfriend

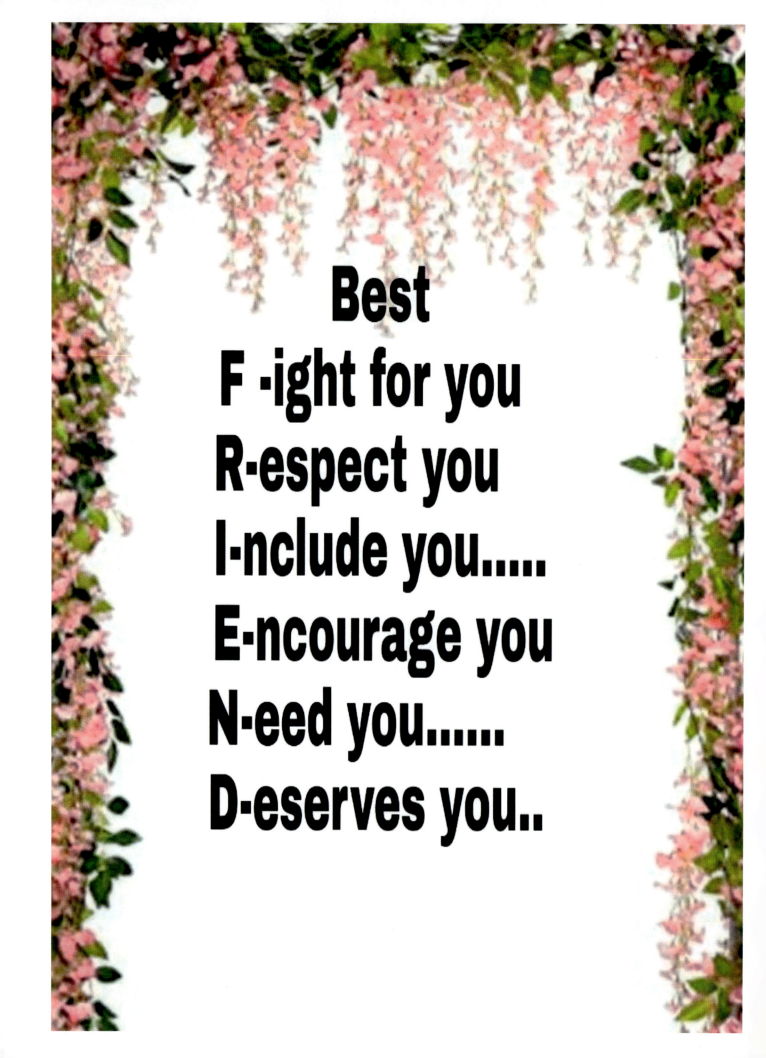

A Bestfriend is someone who loves you unconditionally. Someone who endures your happiness, struggles, and accomplishments.

Advice from Your mom

Love Madison unconditionally. Teach her to love God for he has everlasting love. Allow Madison to have those mommy daughter conversations. Dress her fashionably, while teaching her how to be humble. Practice and teach respect as it will take Madison a long way. Teach her that it's okay to be different. Teach her that Education is the key to success! And common sense is the key to functioning well in life. Put no one before your child! No friend, No enemy, and no man! Only God can see you and Madison through!

The love that you give is what Madison will appreciate the most, so continue love her, as I continue to love you! With Love it pass down generations and generations to come!

Motherhood is not a easy road but God will equip you to drive your path. remember to pray and talk to God daily! Listen to those spiritual songs that will encourage you, such as Hold On. No matter how Madison grow up and start to rebel remember its apart of her growing and Learning, so you continue to teach her. Don't bend or fold, she will thank you later. Remember tell her that you love her and allow your actions to exceed your words. Teach her first at home and continue while she's in public. Monitor the company she keep! Your home preferably! Remember you have family that will back you up. You got this Gabrielle!

I Hereby pronounce Gabrielle Allen to Motherhood! My Beautiful queen, wear your crown and train your princess

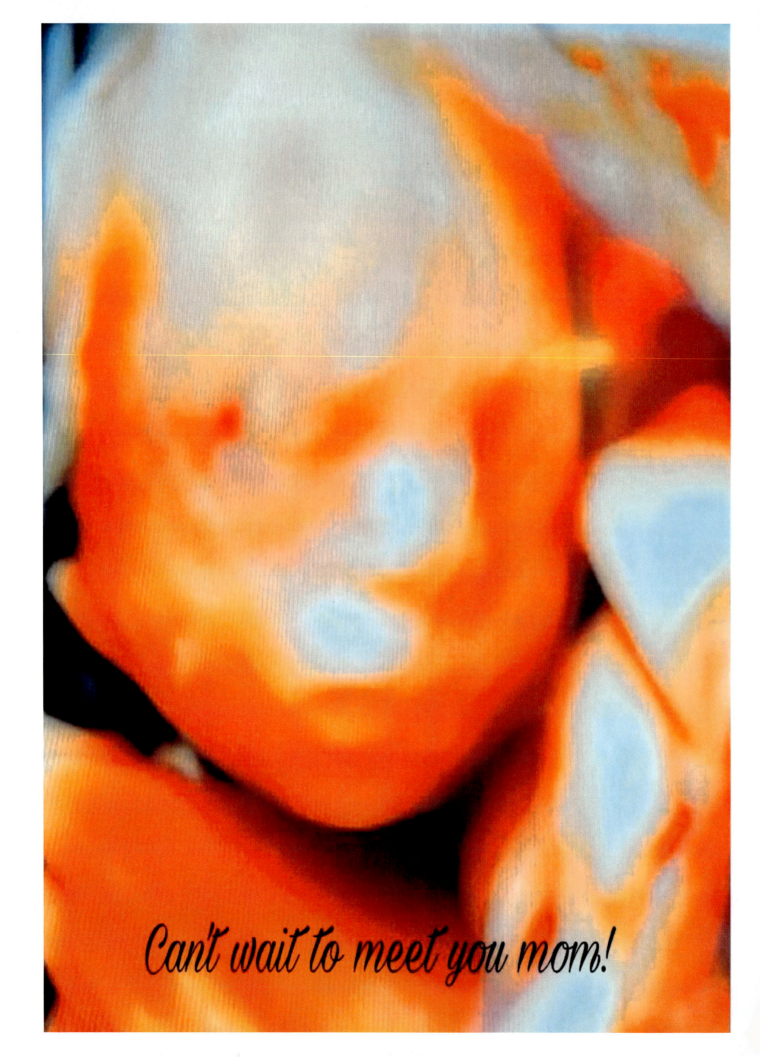

A daughter's Best Friend!

Words of Affirmation to Gabrielle Allen

Words of Affirmation to Gabrielle Allen

Words of Affirmation to Gabrielle Allen

Words of Affirmation to Gabrielle Allen

Words of Affirmation to Gabrielle Allen

Words of Affirmation to Gabrielle Allen

Words of Affirmation to Gabrielle Allen

Words of Affirmation to Gabrielle Allen

Words of Affirmation to Gabrielle Allen

Words of Affirmation to Gabrielle Allen

Words of Affirmation to Gabrielle Allen

Words of Affirmation to Gabrielle Allen

Words of Affirmation to Gabrielle Allen

Words of Affirmation to Gabrielle Allen

Words of Affirmation to Gabrielle Allen

Words of Affirmation to Gabrielle Allen

Words of Affirmation to Gabrielle Allen

Words of Affirmation to Gabrielle Allen

Words of Affirmation to Gabrielle Allen

Words of Affirmation to Gabrielle Allen

Words of Affirmation to Gabrielle Allen